WINCHESTER

❖ *Yesterday and Today* ❖

JOHN BARTON

HALSGROVE

First published in Great Britain in 1998

British Library Cataloguing in Publication Data
A CIP record for this book is available from the British Library

ISBN 1 84114 004 X

HALSGROVE
Halsgrove House
Lower Moor Way
Tiverton
Devon EX16 6SS
Tel: 01884 243242
Fax: 01884 243325

Printed by Bookcraft (Bath) Ltd, Midsomer Norton

Contents

For all those who have recorded

the past and are recording the present

for the benefit of those in the future.

Acknowledgements

This book would not have been possible without the help of several people. I am particularly grateful to Edward Roberts for permission to copy many postcards from his collection, to Philippa Stevens and her staff at the Hampshire Local Studies Library for much assistance with photographs and queries and to Derek Dine for printing the photographs from the library collection. I am also greatly indebted to Phil Yates for information about the streets in old Winchester, to Michael Green for his recollections of streets and shops, to David Fry for permission to use some of his photographs and to Graham Mackay for the loan of postcards. Not least I must thank my daughter Anne-Louise and my son Jeremy for their assistance with taking some of the photographs. Finally I thank the publishers for the opportunity to undertake such an interesting task.

Photographs are reproduced by kind permission of the following:
Edward Roberts: pp. 8, 14, 16, 19, 20, 27, 30, 32, 36, 46, 53, 56, 58, 68, 74, 76, 78, 80, 81, 86, 88, 91, 94
Hampshire County Library: pp. 7, 9, 10, 18, 22, 24, 28, 38, 40, 41, 44, 48, 50, 52, 54, 60, 62, 64, 92, 95
Graham Mackay: pp. 12, 13, 43, 82, 84, 90
David Fry: pp. 8, 34, 42, 72
John Barton: pp. 26, 66, 70

Introduction

There is a peculiar fascination about old photographs, especially those of local street scenes in the early years of the twentieth century. Some towns are now almost unrecognizable compared with a hundred years ago. Even an historic city such as Winchester has seen sweeping changes by redevelopment, especially in the 1950s and 1960s, leaving some streets virtually untouched and others with hardly a single old building left standing. Some of these changes are not necessarily for the better, as will be seen in some of the photographs in this book. Many old buildings have been demolished and replaced by modern ones of dubious architectural merit.

Bygone Winchester is a popular subject, but I have tried to include as far as possible photographs not published before. The majority of the modern photographs in the book have been taken from the same spot as the old photographs were taken. Those that are not quite from the same spot would either have entailed a risk to life and limb or have resulted in a much less interesting picture.

Winchester is not a large city and to avoid having too many photographs of the same street I have included some of the neighbouring villages. In these more rural scenes the changes to buildings are minimal and their interest lies more in the people and vehicles of the time. I hope that this book will prove of interest to those older readers who remember some of the street scenes of long ago and to those younger readers who may often have wondered what Winchester used to look like.

John Barton, Winchester 1998

This photograph of Bar End Road, looking towards Chesil Street, was taken in about 1910. Note the invalid wheelchair and the long dress of the lady in the straw hat. The car is not close enough to identify the make. The house on the left and the nearest of the terraced houses have been demolished and beyond them the wall and trees have made way for a terrace set back from the road. In both photographs the public house on the right is the Heart in Hand.

The Railway Coffee Tavern in Bridge Street, seen here in about 1910, must have been so named after the railway station at Chesil opened in 1885. It is now part of Magdalen Mews. The houses on the extreme right of the photograph have been replaced by buildings set back from the road. The Rising Sun is not greatly altered. St John's Street to the left was the main road into Winchester from the east before Magdalen Hill superseded it.

The eastern end of High Street leading to Bridge Street is seen here from near King Alfred's statue. The Eastgate Restaurant on the left of the picture opened in 1926 (and closed in the early 1960s), so the photograph was taken perhaps in about 1930. There are signs reading 'Cars for hire' and 'Billiards' on the Great Western Hotel, now The Old Monk. The buildings beyond the bridge on the right have been rebuilt and there is now a row of shops between the former Eastgate Restaurant and the bridge.

This photograph shows the part of High Street now named the Broadway before 1901, when King Alfred's statue was erected. It became known as the Broadway in about 1800 after the buildings in the centre of High Street were demolished. Fred Smith, printer, was at No.166, and the Crown and Anchor was owned by the Winchester Brewery Company until it was taken over by Marstons Brewery. Note B.B. Colson's Cheesehill Brewery cart – his premises were near the Winchester Brewery in Cheesehill (now Chesil) Street.

High Street
& Guildhall,
Winchester

This photograph of the Broadway was taken after the extension to the Guildhall was completed in 1893 and before the street lights in the centre were moved to the pavements. The appearance of the Gothic-style Guildhall, completed in 1873, was spoilt by Colson's unfortunate extension. Note the alterations to the ground floor at the near corner. The new photograph shows surprisingly little change to High Street and to the buildings opposite the Guildhall.

The cathedral is seen here about a hundred years ago. From the same spot today it would be obscured by the trees that line the approach. Founded in 1079, Winchester cathedral is the longest medieval church in Europe. It was once about forty feet longer, before the west end of the Norman nave was shortened and rebuilt in the fourteenth century. In the new photograph the statue of a soldier is on the war memorial to the men of the King's Royal Rifle Corps.

Chesil Street was known as Cheesehill Street until about 1915 and was so named on Godson's map of 1750. The war posters and the name Cheesehill indicate that this photograph was taken in about 1915. The half-timbered Chesil rectory is a survival of medieval Winchester, when very few houses were built of stone. The antiques shop of Thomas & Co. became a restaurant in about 1931. Mort's Cycle Depot opened in 1913 or 1914 and it remained a cycle shop until recent times.

This is a rare photograph of City Road, taken in about 1916. The Oriel Temperance Hotel on the left ceased business in 1934. Note the cinema advert on the wall. On the right are a disused chapel and the premises of Redman & Co. (taxis) and H. & C. Cox (greengrocers). On the far corner of Sussex Street can be seen Saunders' cycle shop, which was superseded by the Carfax Hotel in about 1918. The north side of City Road has been largely redeveloped but the south side has undergone little change.

This photograph of Colebrook Street was taken before the redevelopment of the west side in the early 1960s to make way for the Wessex Hotel. It is hard to imagine now how a building so incompatible with its surroundings could be sited within a stone's throw of one of the most historic buildings in England. The signboard towards the far end is that of the Royal Standard public house. In the new photograph Market Lane is on the immediate right.

Eastgate Street in about 1907 is recognizable as the same street today, even with a few changes. The imposing block of houses on the right has been replaced by a less attractive building – one would be surprised were it otherwise. The best houses in the street are out of sight to the photographer's left. Eastgate Street is relatively new in the historic context of Winchester: it was laid out in the middle of the nineteenth century after the demolition of Eastgate House and was at first named High Street, Eastgate.

The fifteenth-century Butter Cross, seen here in about 1900, was saved from removal in 1770 by angry citizens. Very little of it is original – it was restored in 1865. It should be called the High Cross, but came by its more familiar name presumably because of the market that was here. The City Cross Refreshment Rooms closed in about 1904 and were succeeded by Allen's the confectioners. The jettied timber-framed building (until recently the Spinning Wheel) is probably fourteenth century.

This view of High Street was taken between 1929, when the Talbot Hotel replaced the Star Inn, and 1934, when the policemen in white coats on traffic duty were replaced by traffic-lights. Warrens then published the *Hampshire Observer*, which ceased publication in 1957. The business of Robert Marks, cutler at No. 86, was run by Mr Coombes, whose daughter owned the Commercial School. On the south side Whitwams have been in business since 1909. Page and Phillips (No. 67) were fishmongers and poulterers. At that date all London to Southampton traffic passed through Winchester.

This photograph shows High Street in about 1902. On the left are Hunt & Co., chemists since 1861 (the shop is now on display in the City Museum), Teague & King's music saloon, Clifton & Sons, clothiers and outfitters, and Kaines, poulterer. The shop on the right at No. 103 is T.A. Brown & Sons, hosiers (now Debenhams). The Guildhall (now Lloyds Bank) was built in 1713; the clock is a replica of the original. The front of God Begot House is a restoration but the interior is very old.

This view of High Street was taken from the top of the West Gate early this century (there are no motor vehicles in sight). John Hodder at No. 80, cabinet-maker, upholsterer and carpet dealer, ceased business in 1914. The buildings on the right, hidden by scaffolding in the new photograph, are essentially unchanged. The new building on the immediate left is the council's Mottisfont Court, in stark contrast with the architecture farther down High Street.

Mr A. Faithfull, coal merchant, stands outside his premises in Hyde Street in about 1907. The business closed in the 1940s. The new photograph shows that the building is not much altered. The stone and brick house on the right was demolished in the 1960s to construct a new road (Hyde Place). Otherwise much of this part of Hyde Street remains unchanged.

The George Hotel was demolished for road widening in 1956 so this photograph of Jewry Street was taken between 1953, when Burtol Cleaners opened in High Street, and 1956. The George had closed as a hotel in 1939 and did not reopen after the war. There had been a George Inn or Hotel here for about five hundred years. The buildings on the left – Drake and Gorham, electrical engineers, Michael Harrington, bookseller, and Stone, hairdresser – have also been pulled down. Barclays Bank opened in 1959 on the site of the George Hotel.

This photograph of Jewry Street was taken in about 1916 (note the soldiers' canteen sign on the left). The old gaol, built in 1805, was occupied by Stopher's, and is now the Old Gaolhouse tavern. The Congregational church was built in 1853. Rider's studio at No. 11 is also now occupied by the Old Gaolhouse. The main business of Matthews and Sons ('cars for hire') was furniture and carpets. Jewry Street was the home of Jewish traders until they were expelled in 1290.

The Market Hotel in Jewry Street opened in 1850 and closed in 1912. Note its splendid wrought-iron balcony. The Theatre Royal succeeded the Market Hotel, opening in August 1914. In 1920 it started to show films and two years later became solely a cinema, continuing as such until 1974. This photograph was taken in about 1907. Note that the hotel catered for the Cyclists Touring Club (CTC) and the National Cyclists Union (NCU). When the new photograph was taken the theatre was once again being renovated.

The Corn Exchange in Jewry Street (now the County Library) was built in 1836–8 of yellow brick and white ashlar to the design of Owen Carter. The Tuscan portico was probably modelled on that of St Paul's church in Covent Garden. Before opening as a library in 1936 it had been occupied by the Regent cinema and a restaurant. The hut on the pavement on the right was perhaps a cab office; at least it looks more attractive than the modern bus shelter.

Kingsgate Street is little changed since this photograph was taken before the First World War. The house on the right (No. 70) has two of the best examples of Georgian bow-windows in Winchester. The first-floor bow-window seen in the new photograph dates only from the early part of this century but looks older. A walk along Kingsgate Street is a rewarding exercise for devotees of Georgian architecture.

The King's Head public house in Little Minster Street closed in about 1934. The early (Morris?) car is standing outside what was then the Minster Garage, which was demolished in the 1960s. The inn sign on the left is at the rear entrance of the Old Vine Inn. The five-bayed building beyond the King's Head is recognizably the same one. The railings guarding the passage to The Square may have been taken for scrap during the war.

All the houses on the east side of Lower Brook Street have been replaced, but Garden Lane remains. The photographs show how the street looked before and after the redevelopment of the 1960s. Each of the three Brook streets once had a brook or stream flowing down its centre. Lower Brook Street was in medieval times known as *Tannerestret* (its continuation is still named Tanner Street). The near lamp-post seems to be the same one. For a change the new houses are an improvement on the old ones.

This photograph shows Market Lane not long before the Wessex Hotel was built in the early 1960s. The premises of the Winchester Industrial Co-operative Society, Cooper Bros. (mercantile stores) and Sherriff and Ward, which all fronted on to High Street, had been there since before the First World War. Paternoster Row turned off Market Lane on the left of the photograph and now passes underneath the Wessex Hotel.

Parchment Street is seen here in about 1905. Remarkably the large painted sign 'Carriage and Motor Works' survives after more than ninety years. The owners, Lane and Son, ceased trading in 1906 and the business was taken over by a Mr Short. The *Hampshire Observer* newspaper moved to Staple Gardens in 1905 and ceased publication in 1957. Parchment Street was formerly known as *Flesmangerestret* (Fleshmonger Street) until the name was transferred to St Peter Street.

The Peninsula Barracks as seen here were rebuilt after a disastrous fire in 1894. The building had been designed by Christopher Wren as a palace for Charles II but was left unfinished on his death in 1685. Later known as the King's House, it became a barracks in 1796. After the fire it was rebuilt in 1899–1902 as three separate buildings using some of the columns from the old building. Vacated by the army a few years ago, the buildings have now been divided into luxury apartments.

The Pentice in High Street is pictured in the 1900s. Pentice is an alternative and somewhat earlier name for a penthouse. Note the Tuscan columns, and the barge-boards on Nos. 31 and 33–35. Shops include on the left R.G. Gifford, corn and seed merchant, and on the right E. Butcher & Son, outfitters and hatters, which is now Holland & Barrett. The shop-front of T. Foster, tobacconist at No. 34 (now Tie Rack), was given to the City Museum in 1980. This business had only two proprietors in over a hundred years.

This is St Cross Road looking towards the city in about 1912, and in the distance is Stanmore Lane junction. At that date this part of it was named Front Street. (Back Street runs parallel to it behind the houses on the right.) So the Wheatsheaf public house in the distance on the left was then No. 31 Front Street but is now No. 104 St Cross Road. Most of the other buildings on either side are little changed.

This view of St George's Street was taken before 1956 from the junction with St Peter Street. It is hard to appreciate now just how narrow St George's Street was. It had served since medieval times as a sort of service road to High Street. The house on the corner on the left (No. 23 St Peter Street) has an eighteenth-century front, which may be later than the rest of the building.

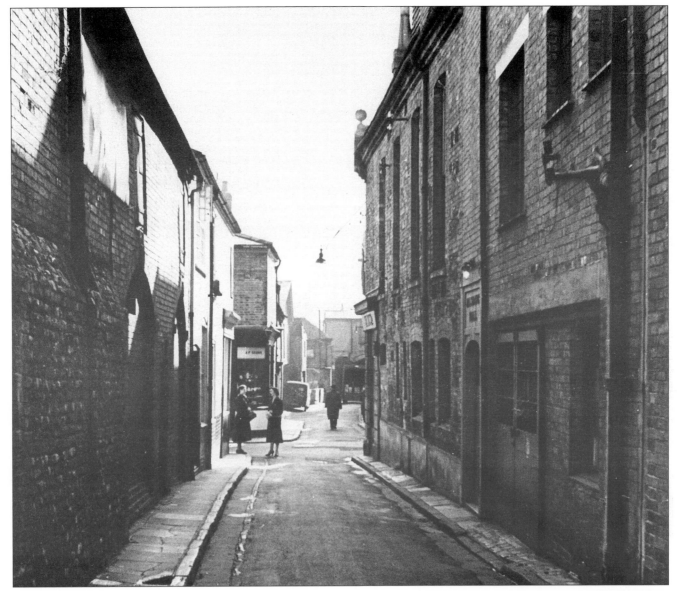

Another view of St George's Street before it was widened in 1956–7. The Masonic Hall, now occupied by W.H. Smith and Son, is recognizable (note the finial on the roof), but all the buildings on the north side of the street have been demolished. On the far corner of Parchment Street was the shop of A.P. Sharpe, jeweller, and on the near corner was the Post Office Tavern.

Southgate Street was widened in 1934 and in these photographs taken at the junction with High Street it can be seen by how much. The Black Swan Hotel was demolished at the same time as the road-widening, and the corner building (now set further back) is occupied by the Framing Centre. The opposite side was once known as Hayward's Corner, from the name of the shop-owner, a tobacconist.

Nos. 23 and 24 The Square obviously formed a single architectural design. Note Chalkley's silver fish sign. Magrath's bookshop was in business there only from 1905 to 1906, according to *Warren's Guide*, so this photograph was taken at that time. The City Museum building opened in 1903. The Eclipse Inn was once the rectory of St Lawrence's church; it was so named because of the Sun Inn that used to be nearby. The plaster covering the timber framing was removed in the 1920s when the building was restored.

Upper Brook Street has had an eventful history in recent years. After demolition of the buildings in the photograph the area became a car-park and is now occupied by the Brooks Centre. The large white building on the end was the Queen's Head public house. In the late eighteenth century it was the head-quarters of the Winchester–London carriers. It stood where the road now is. The new photograph neatly illustrates the fact that everywhere we walk today we have to avoid street furniture – railings, seats, signs – and everywhere we look there are names, signs and advertisements.

The Fountain, Winchester.

This photograph of the Upper High Street junction shows the drinking-fountain erected in 1880 to commemorate a doctor named Littlehales. Near it can be seen the public toilets (underground). The fountain was moved to Clifton Terrace in 1935. The Castle public house on the corner of Sussex Street, now Charles' House, seems to be little changed. The buildings on the right were replaced by the County Council buildings.

The Monument Upper High Street, Winchester.   4659.

The Plague Monument in Upper High Street was erected in 1759 by the Society of Natives to mark the spot where money was exchanged for goods at the time of the 1665 plague. The shop of Carter the confectioner was numbered as part of Upper High Street and was in business there from 1908 to 1922. The photograph was probably taken before the First World War.

Wales Street has changed more than almost any other street in Winchester since this photograph was taken in about 1902, when the Wheatsheaf Inn was at No. 4 and the Ship Inn next door at No. 5. By 1910 only the Wheatsheaf was still in business, and in 1916 it changed its name to the Ship Inn. The present Ship Inn is the same former combined building. Compared with its former tranquillity Wales Street is now a busy route for vehicles to and from Winnall.

This photograph of the Weirs was taken, to judge by the dress of the people, in about 1900. It is likely that the row of houses on the right, just north of Wharf Mill, was demolished in the 1940s – it is not shown on the 1951 Ordnance Survey map. The terrace of houses just visible by the path on the left was knocked down in the 1930s. Note the wooden railings in the foreground: although they have been renewed they still follow the same curves.

The West Gate, photographed in about 1902 from High Street. The business of J. Salter and Sons ('Purveyor of meat to the Queen') opened in the second half of the nineteenth century and lasted until the 1950s. It supplied meat to Queen Victoria at Osborne House. The Plume of Feathers was demolished in 1938 to make way for the Council offices, which finally opened in 1959. The West Gate was bypassed in 1956, not before time.

This view of the West Gate from the west shows the other side of the Plume of Feathers, which flanked it on the north. The west front of the thirteenth-century West Gate was restored in the late fourteenth century. It has lost its parapet but retains its machicolations, from which objects of an unpleasant nature could be dropped on attackers. The new photograph emphasizes the contrast between the West Gate and the modern buildings on the corner of Tower Street.

This picture of Wharf Hill is thought to date from the First World War. Although the Dog and Duck public house closed in 1923 and the building was demolished in about 1938, the Black Boy Inn is still there. Wharf Hill led to Blackbridge Wharf at the north end of the Itchen Navigation. This canal transported mainly coal from Southampton and was last used in 1869. Wharf Mill is in the centre background of the new photograph.

In this view of Winchester, taken from St Giles's Hill, the entire length of High Street can be followed. The most important street of the city for close on two thousand years, it is not quite as straight as it must once have been. The important landmarks have not altered but there are many minor changes if one looks closely at the city's buildings. In the new photograph the tall building that mars the skyline is the County Police Headquarters of 1962–5. The Wessex Hotel and the County Council buildings are also all too prominent.

This photograph shows Worthy Road as seen from the end of Hyde Street. At the time of this photograph (about 1912) Worthy Road-Hyde Street was the main thoroughfare and Worthy Lane to the left only a narrow road. Today Worthy Road-Worthy Lane takes precedence over Hyde Street. The large white house (Danesacre) is now hidden by trees.

This photograph was taken in about 1908 at the junction of the Winchester–Southampton road with the road to the village of Compton, looking towards Winchester. The road is on the line of the Roman road from Winchester to Bitterne. The old forge on the right was demolished in the 1920s, by a motor car it is said. Until 1869 an inn named The Chequers stood on the corner on the left, since when Compton has had no public house.

This rural scene was taken in about 1905 at Easton, at the far end of the village on the Avington road, looking back towards the village. The thatched cottage on the left is still there but not those on the right. The old man on the left is carrying various belongings, including implements of some sort, while the more prosperous-looking man on the right sports a small straw hat. It was customary for the old photographers to 'pose' people to make a good picture.

The sixteenth-century timber-framed Chestnut Horse Inn at Easton is pictured here some time after 1910 (when the licensee was Mr Collard). It seems that alcohol was not the only refreshment offered then. Easton once had a blacksmith, two bakers, two general stores, a post office and sundry other tradesmen. Since 1970 it has not had even one shop, but its two public houses are still flourishing.

This photograph shows the main road at Hursley in about 1905. The King's Head public house can be seen in the distance on the left (the licensee then was Arthur Russell). The village hall on the right is obscured by trees in the new photograph. Note the three tall eighteenth-century chimneys, each with a different design.

The main road at Hursley is seen here in about 1900. The large house with three chimneys is the Dolphin public house (the licensee in 1902 was Josiah Perry). The twin-gabled house in the distance on the right was built in 1897. The blacksmith's shop in the centre distance continued as such until quite recent times (the 1970s), and is now an antiques shop.

Here at Kings Worthy in about 1930 the road to London is on the left and the road to Alresford on the right. As most London to Southampton traffic came this way the junction was considered busy enough to warrant having an R.A.C. patrolman on duty. Today, although it is much busier, there is not even a set of traffic lights at the junction. The nearest buildings have all disappeared (the one on the left was a chapel or meeting house), but the houses behind them still exist. At this date the London road ran in a fairly straight line into the village as far as the church.

The eighteenth-century Cart and Horses public house at Kings Worthy is seen here in about 1930. Note the early Austin Seven, the motor coaches typical of that period, the tricycle possibly delivering meat or bread, and what looks like a petrol pump between the two motor coaches. The Cart and Horses must have been a popular stop for people travelling between London and Southampton.

Littleton in 1906. The local children, neatly lined up by the photographer, are all respectably dressed, as even the children of poor parents generally were in those days. The main change in the scene today is that the road is now made up. The White House on the right was a medieval hall house built in about 1500 with four bays, one of which was the hall.

The blacksmith's forge at Otterbourne, known to have been working in the early nineteenth century, is seen here in about 1905, when the blacksmith was a lady by the name of Betsy Comely! It continued as a forge until the 1920s, when the smith was Ernie Monckton. It is now the Old Forge restaurant. The far end of the row of cottages has been demolished, and there are more trees now.

This photograph of Otterbourne village may have been taken from a house that no longer exists. The first house on the right (Elderfield) was the home of the prolific author Charlotte Mary Yonge, and it remains unaltered today. She was born at Otterbourne House, a large house not visible in the photograph. In the clump of trees by the roadside on the left is Rose Cottage, which was owned by Charlotte Yonge. Today, all the houses in the earlier picture are hidden by trees that have grown in the intervening years.

This scene in Shawford dates from about 1905, over twenty years after Shawford station was opened (in 1882). The Bridge Hotel, formerly called the Bridge Inn, once kept horses for working the barges on the Itchen Navigation. Apart from minor alterations both the inn and the buildings on the right are little changed. The mission hall was opened in 1892 and ceased to hold meetings in 1956. As in other villages, the main change is that the road has been made up.

Twyford crossroads is pictured here probably at the turn of the century. The previous post office was situated opposite the Phoenix Inn. The exterior of this building is unchanged apart from its coat of white paint. The village hall and some modern buildings, including a surgery, have been built in the field in the background. No doubt residents of Twyford wish it was as peaceful here today as it was a hundred years ago.

This view of the main road through Twyford village, not yet made up, dates from before the First World War. Note the sign on the Phoenix Inn: 'Lady Cyclists House'. An early concession to the feminist movement? The Phoenix was an inn in 1690 but is now mainly nineteenth century. Mr Hewlett took over as licensee in about 1900. The far end of the inn has been demolished but otherwise not much has changed. The two men are outside Carter's forge; the Carter family owned the forge from the early nineteenth century to 1936.

When this photograph was taken Weeke was much more of a village than it is today. Development began in the nineteenth century but in 1911 the population of Weeke Without (outside the walls) was only about a hundred. It is fortunate that the old parish church of St Matthew has survived, as has the village pond and its railings, but the nearest house on the right has been demolished.

About the Author

John Barton has lived in Winchester for over thirty years. He has written five other books on Hampshire, including *The Visitor's Guide to Hampshire and the Isle of Wight* and *Hidden Hampshire*.

A retired cartographical surveyor, he now divides his time between writing books and antiquarian bookselling. His other interests include travelling and croquet.